MW01329694
THIS NOTEBOOK BELONGS TO

And now, the end is near, as you've just faced, the final page turn...

Fear not, be not afraid...

More of what you love is just one scan away!

Designs of note!®

available at amazon

Made in the USA
Columbia, SC
26 June 2025

59899529R00057